Based on the best-selling piano method by Kenneth Baker.

THE COMPLETE PIANO PLAYER
BOB DYLAN

All words and music by Bob Dylan.

HAL•LEONARD®

Exclusive distributors:
Hal Leonard
7777 West Bluemound Road
Milwaukee, WI 53213
Email: info@halleonard.com

Hal Leonard Europe Limited
42 Wigmore Street
Marylebone, London, W1U 2RY
Email: info@halleonardeurope.com

Hal Leonard Australia Pty. Ltd.
4 Lentara Court
Cheltenham, Victoria, 3192 Australia
Email: info@halleonard.com.au

This book © Copyright 2014 by Hal Leonard.
Order No. AM1008326
ISBN: 978-1-78305-448-0

Arranged by Derek Jones.
Processed by Paul Ewers Music Design.
Edited by Ruth Power.

Printed in the EU.

www.halleonard.com

All Along The Watchtower

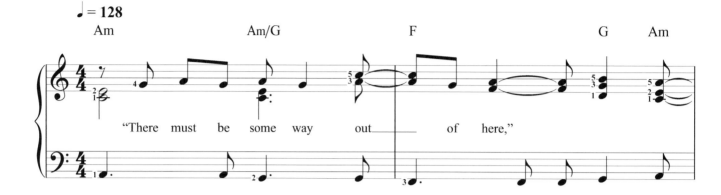

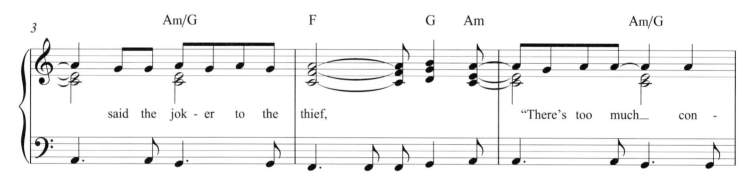

4

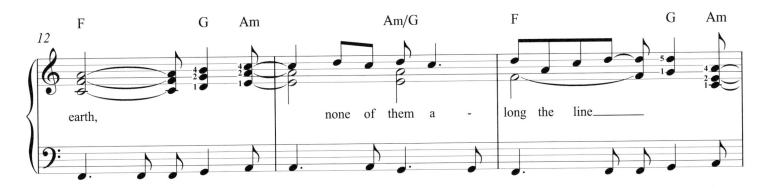

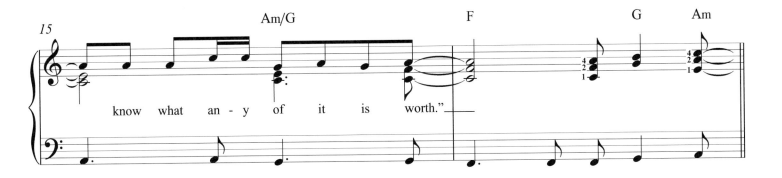

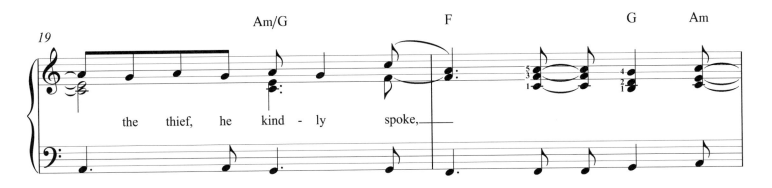

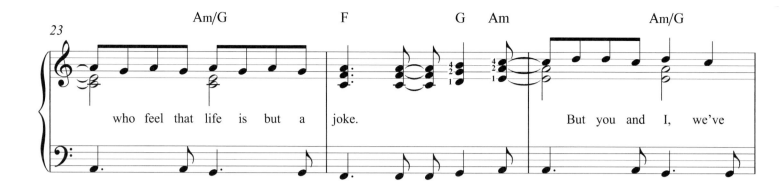

who feel that life is but a joke. But you and I, we've

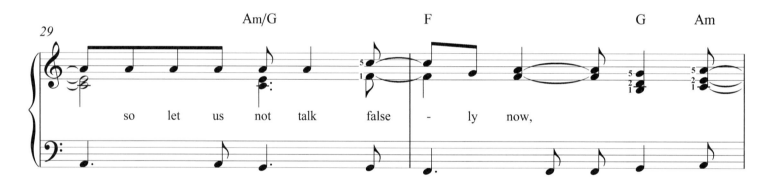

been through that, and this is not our fate, ____

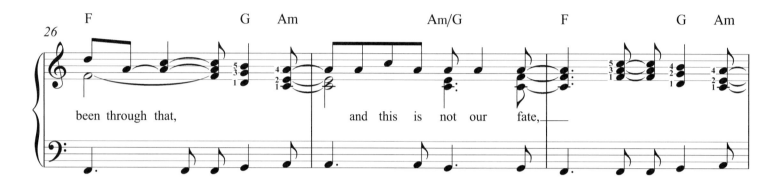

so let us not talk false - ly now,

the hour is get - ting late." ____

All a - long the watch - tow - er, ____ princ - es kept the view, ___

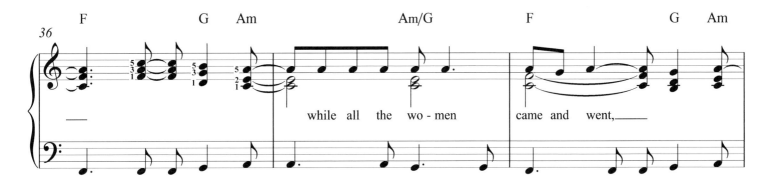

while all the wo - men came and went,____

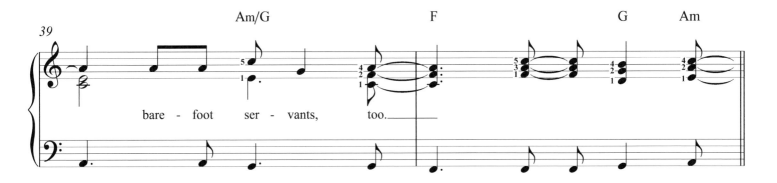

bare - foot ser - vants, too.____

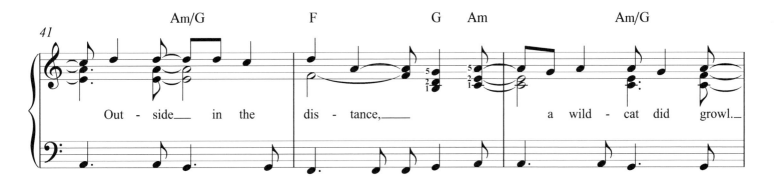

Out - side____ in the dis - tance,____ a wild - cat did growl.____

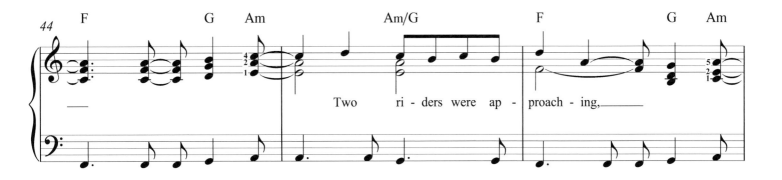

Two ri - ders were ap - proach - ing,____

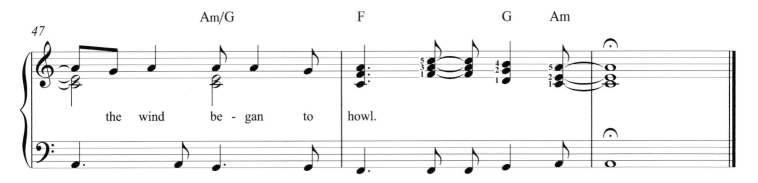

the wind be - gan to howl.

Blowin' In The Wind

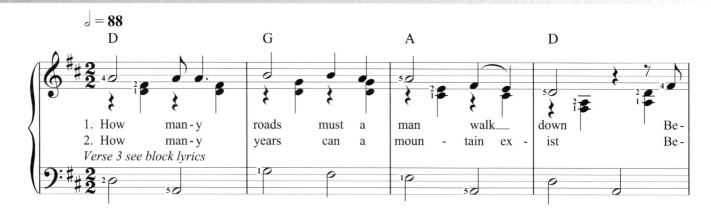

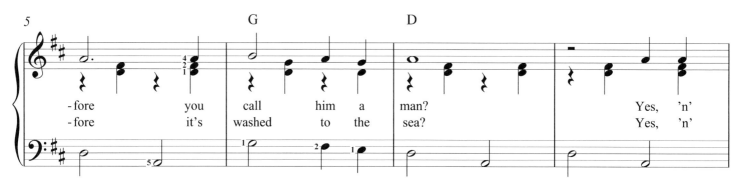

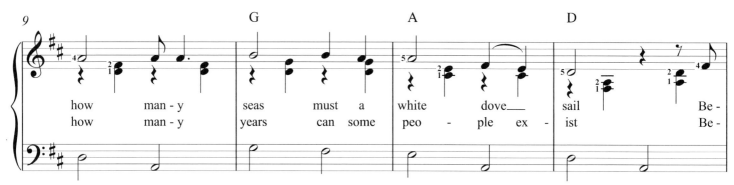

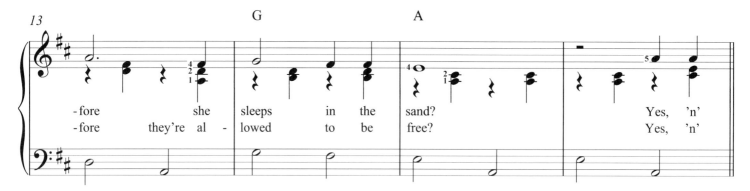

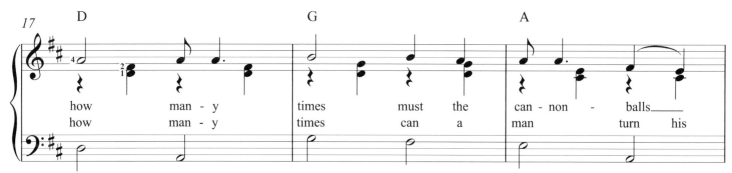

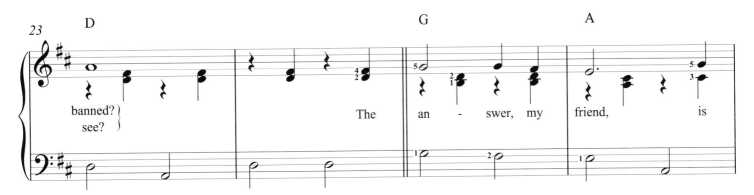

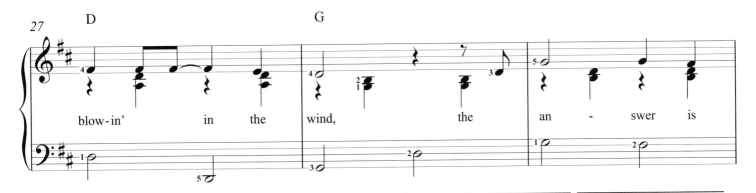

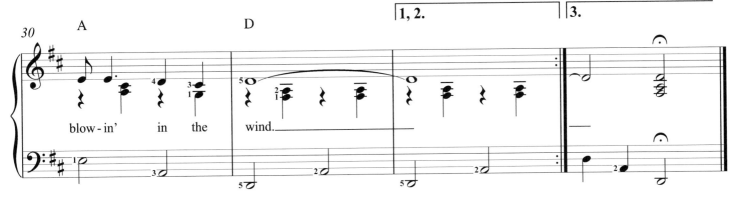

Verse 3
How many times must a man look up
Before he can see the sky?
Yes, 'n' how many ears must one man have
Before he can hear people cry?
Yes, 'n' how many deaths will it take till he knows
That too many people have died?
The answer, my friend, is blowin' in the wind
The answer is blowin' in the wind

Forever Young

Verse 3
May your hands always be busy
May your feet always be swift
May you have a strong foundation
When the winds of changes shift
May your heart always be joyful
May your song always be sung
May you stay forever young
Forever young, forever young
May you stay forever young

I Shall Be Released

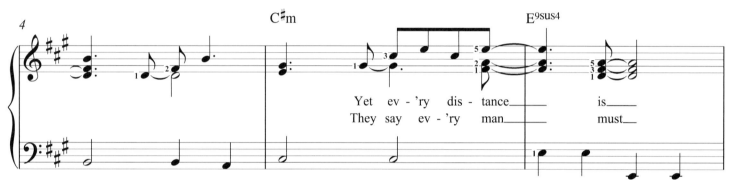

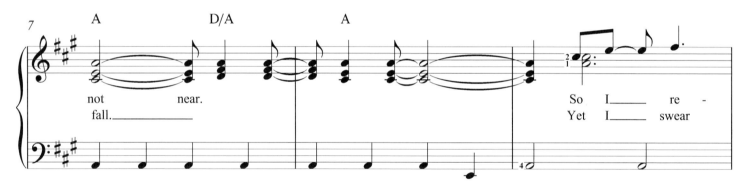

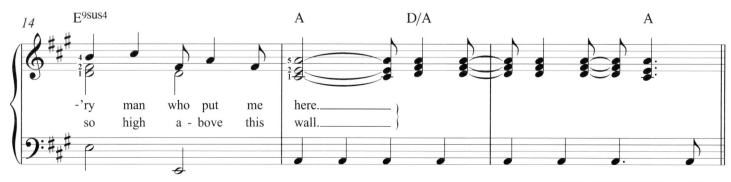

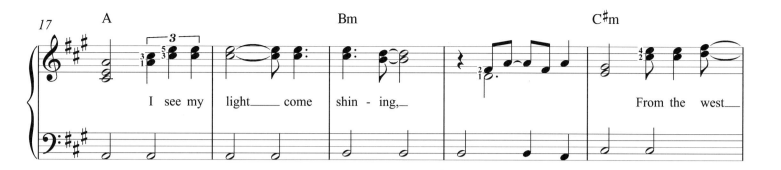

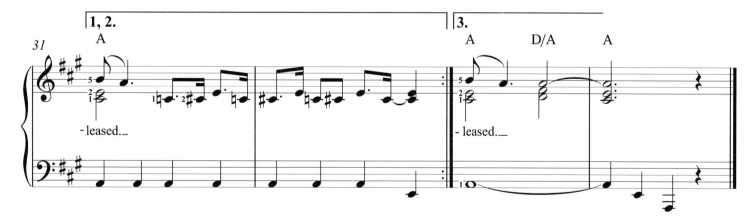

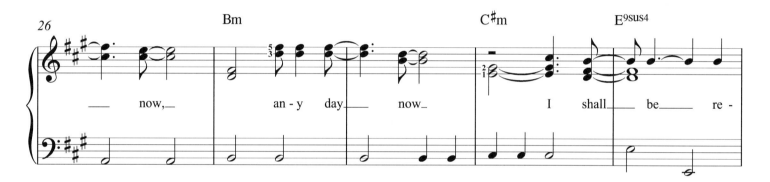

Verse 3
Standing next to me in this lonely crowd
Is a man who swears he's not to blame
All day long I hear him shout so loud
Crying out that he was framed
I see my light come shining
From the west unto the east
Any day now, any day now
I shall be released

If Not For You

♩ = 140

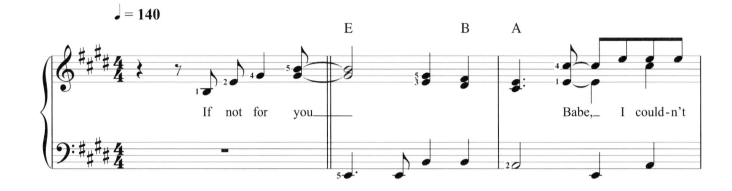

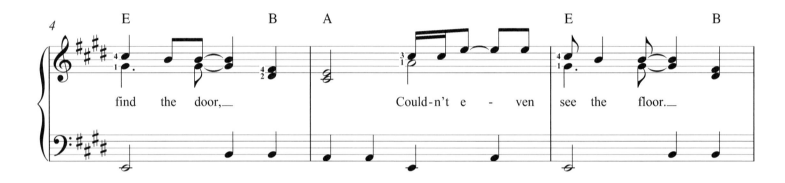

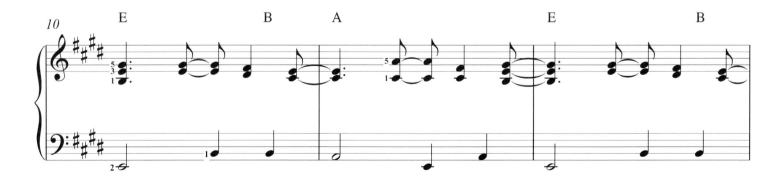

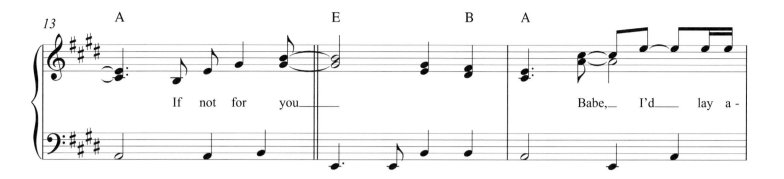

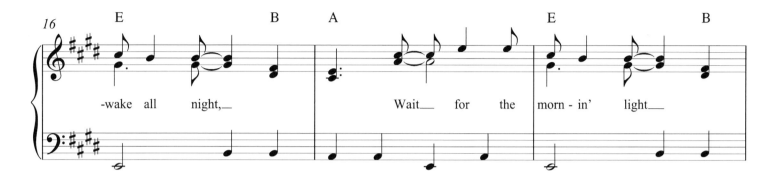

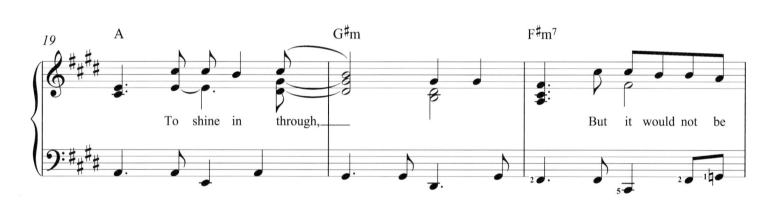

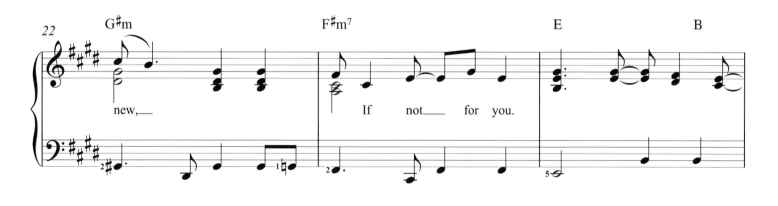

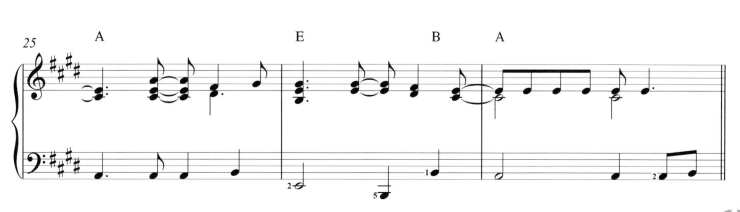

15

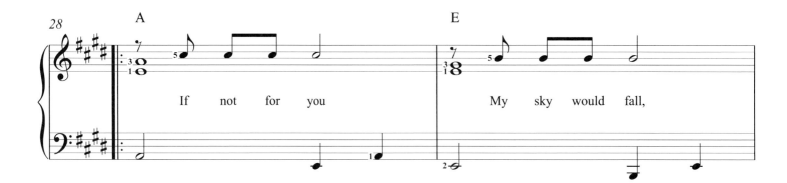

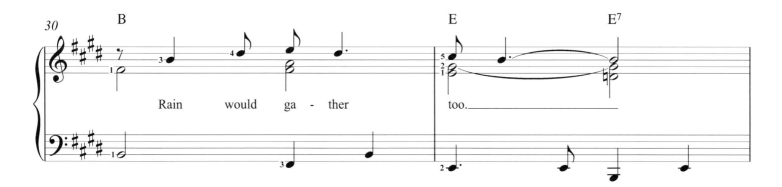

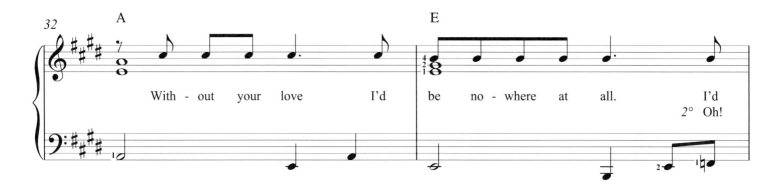

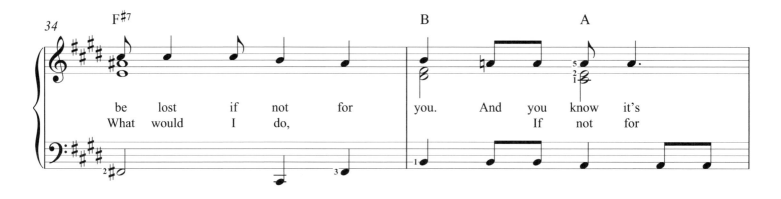

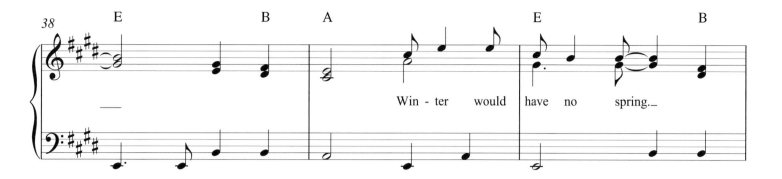

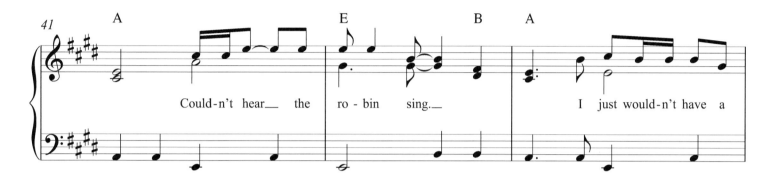

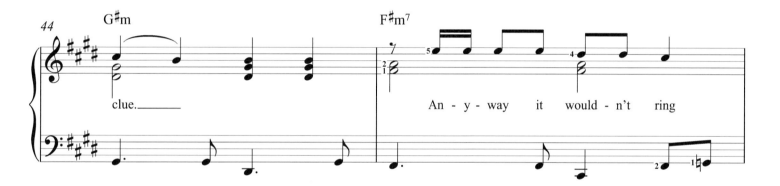

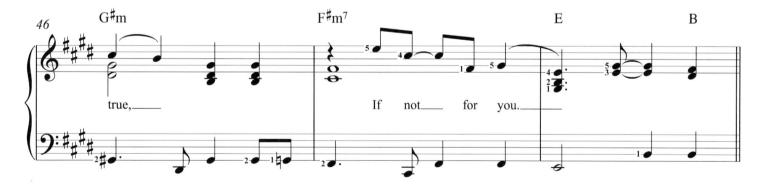

Repeat ad lib. to fade

It Ain't Me Babe

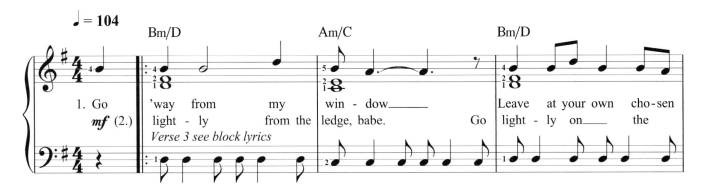

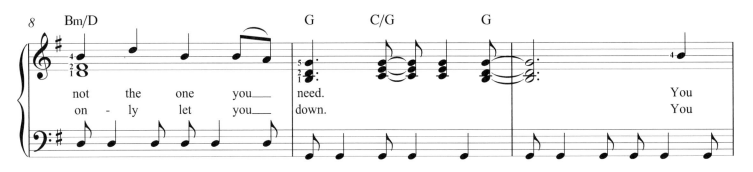

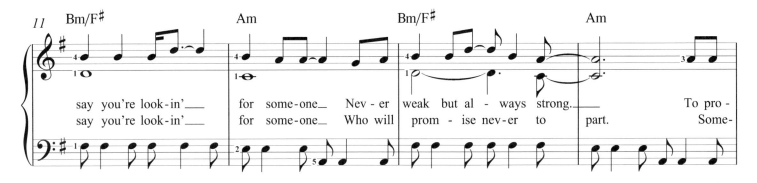

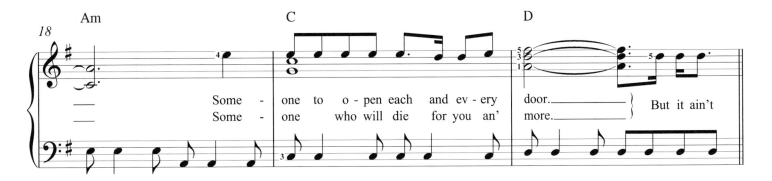

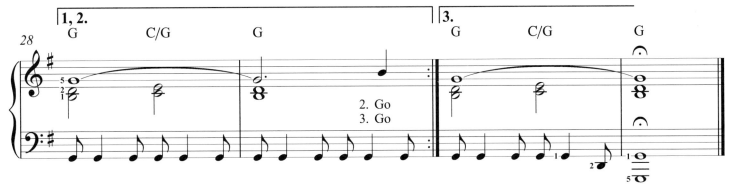

Verse 3
Go melt back into the night, babe
Everything inside is made of stone
There's nothing in here moving
An' anyway I'm not alone
You say you're lookin' for someone
Who'll pick you up each time you fall
To gather flowers constantly
An' to come each time you call
A lover for your life an' nothing more
But it ain't me, babe
No, no, no, it ain't me, babe
It ain't me you're lookin' for, babe

Knockin' On Heaven's Door

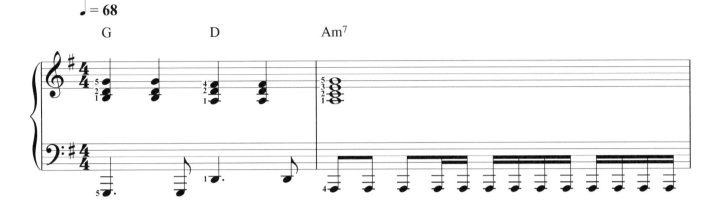

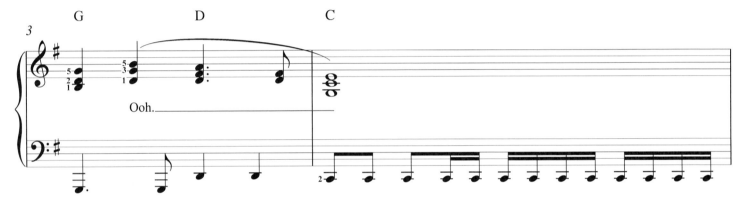

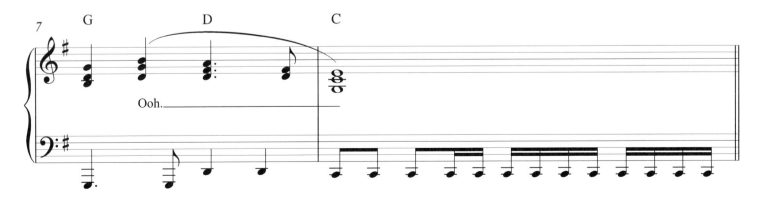

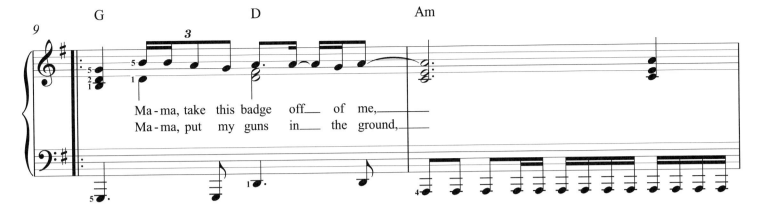

G   D   Am

Ma - ma, take this badge off____ of me,____
Ma - ma, put my guns in____ the ground,____

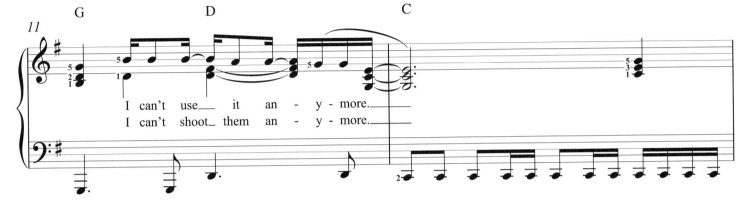

G   D   C

I can't use____ it an - y - more.
I can't shoot____ them an - y - more.

G   D   Am⁷

It's get - tin' dark,____ too dark for me to see,____
That long black cloud____ is com - in' down,____

G   D   C

I feel like I'm knock - in' on hea - ven's door.____
I feel like I'm knock - in' on hea - ven's door.____

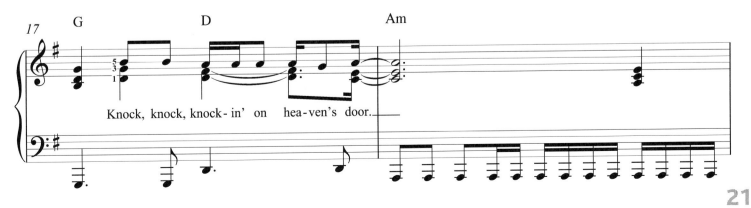

G   D   Am

Knock, knock, knock - in' on hea - ven's door.____

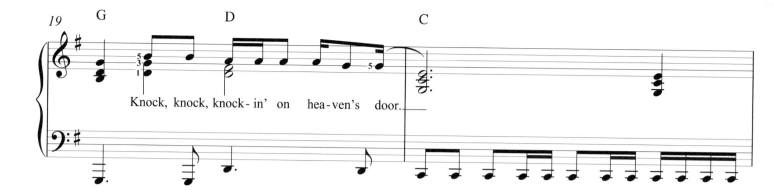

Knock, knock, knock-in' on hea-ven's door.

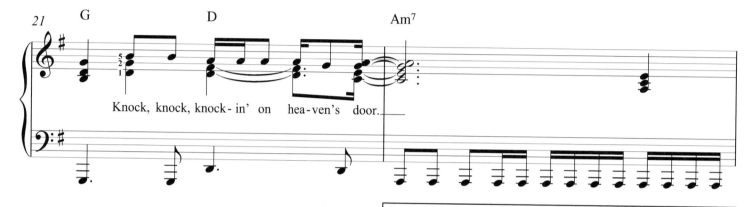

Knock, knock, knock-in' on hea-ven's door.

1.

Knock, knock, knock-in' on hea-ven's door.

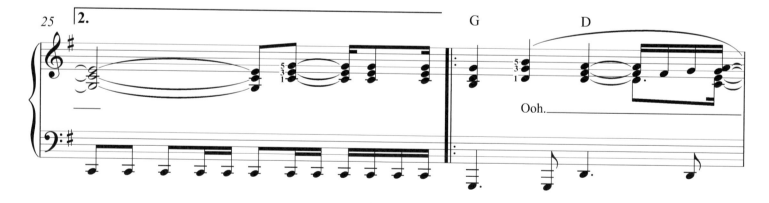

2.

Ooh.

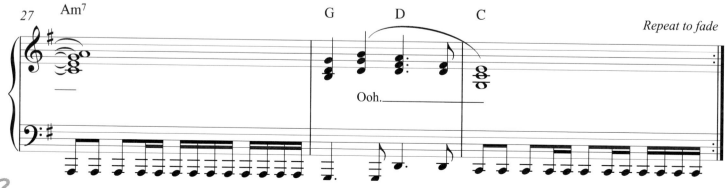

Repeat to fade

Ooh.

Lay, Lady, Lay

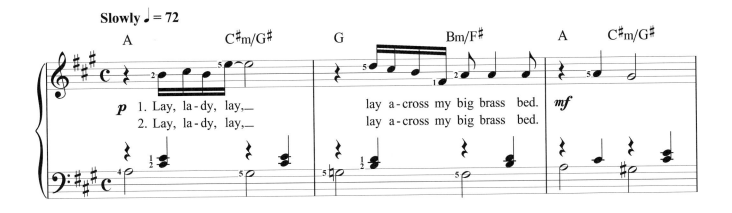

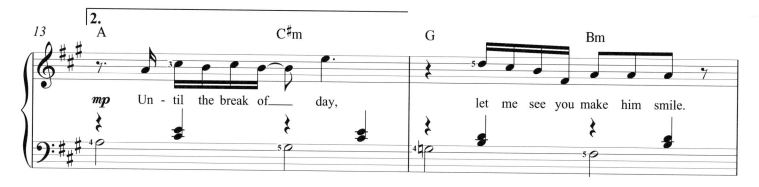

D.S. al Coda

24

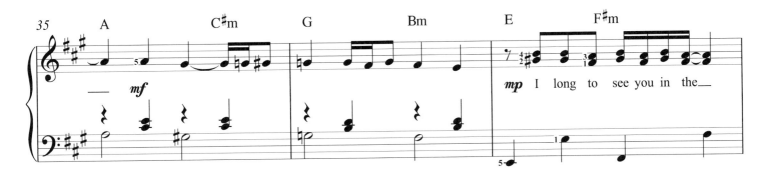

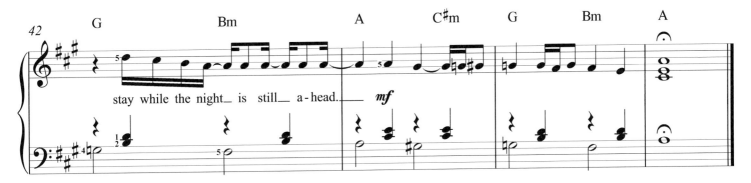

Mr. Tambourine Man

-gle jan - gle morn - ing I'll come fol - low - in'

you. Though I know
Verses 2-4 see block lyrics

___ that eve - nin's em - pire___ has re - turned in - to sand,

___ Van - ished from___ my hand, Left me blind -

- ly here___ to stand___ but still___ not sleep - ing.___

My wea - ri - ness___ a - maz - es me,___ I'm

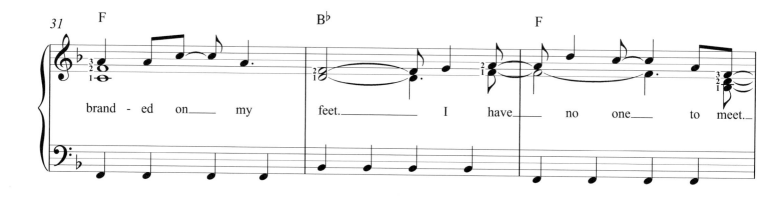

brand - ed on___ my feet.___ I have___ no one___ to meet.___

___ And the an - cient emp - ty street's___ too dead___ for dream-

Play 4 times then **D.C. al Coda**

Coda

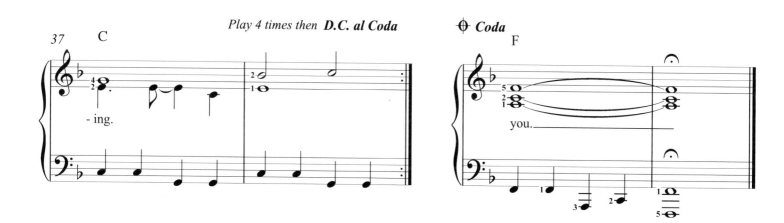

-ing.

you.___

See following page for additional lyrics.

Verse 2

Hey! Mr. Tambourine Man, play a song for me
I'm not sleepy and there is no place I'm going to
Hey! Mr. Tambourine Man, play a song for me
In the jingle jangle morning I'll come followin' you

Take me on a trip upon your magic swirlin' ship
My senses have been stripped, my hands can't feel to grip
My toes too numb to step
Wait only for my boot heels to be wanderin'
I'm ready to go anywhere, I'm ready for to fade
Into my own parade, cast your dancing spell my way
I promise to go under it

Verse 3

Hey! Mr. Tambourine Man, play a song for me
I'm not sleepy and there is no place I'm going to
Hey! Mr. Tambourine Man, play a song for me
In the jingle jangle morning I'll come followin' you

Though you might hear laughin', spinnin', swingin' madly across the sun
It's not aimed at anyone, it's just escapin' on the run
And but for the sky there are no fences facin'
And if you hear vague traces of skippin' reels of rhyme
To your tambourine in time, it's just a ragged clown behind
I wouldn't pay it any mind
It's just a shadow you're seein' that he's chasing

Verse 4

Hey! Mr. Tambourine Man, play a song for me
I'm not sleepy and there is no place I'm going to
Hey! Mr. Tambourine Man, play a song for me
In the jingle jangle morning I'll come followin' you

Then take me disappearin' through the smoke rings of my mind
Down the foggy ruins of time, far past the frozen leaves
The haunted, frightened trees, out to the windy beach
Far from the twisted reach of crazy sorrow
Yes, to dance beneath the diamond sky with one hand waving free
Silhouetted by the sea, circled by the circus sands
With all memory and fate driven deep beneath the waves
Let me forget about today until tomorrow

Hey! Mr. Tambourine Man, play a song for me
I'm not sleepy and there is no place I'm going to
Hey! Mr. Tambourine Man, play a song for me
In the jingle jangle morning I'll come followin' you

Quinn The Eskimo (The Mighty Quinn)

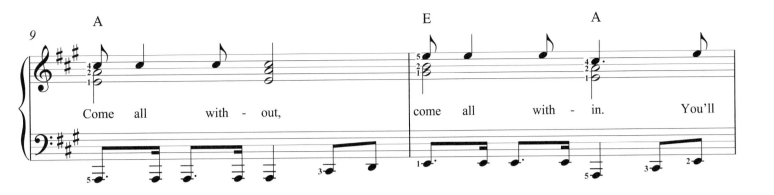

Come all with-out, come all with-in. You'll

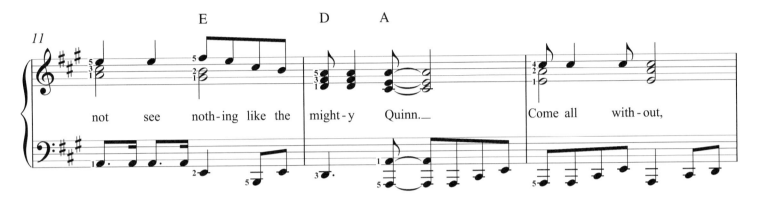

not see noth-ing like the might-y Quinn.___ Come all with-out,

come all with-in. You'll not see noth-ing like the might-y Quinn.___

Play 3 times

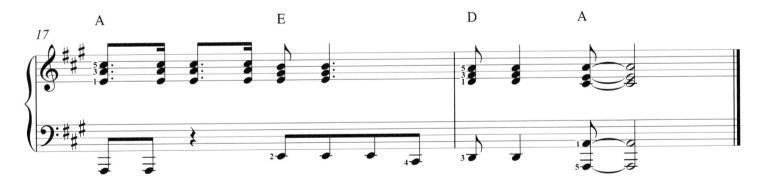

Verse 3
A cat's meow and a cow's moo, I can recite 'em all
Just tell me where it hurts yuh, honey
And I'll tell you who to call
Nobody can get no sleep
There's someone on ev'ryone's toes
But when Quinn the Eskimo gets here
Ev'rybody's gonna wanna doze
Come all without, come all within
You'll not see nothing like the mighty Quinn

Tangled Up In Blue

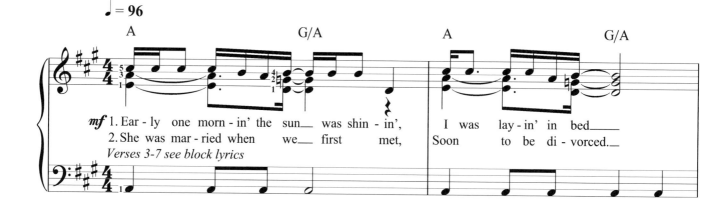

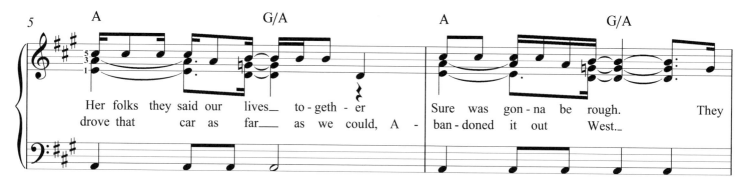

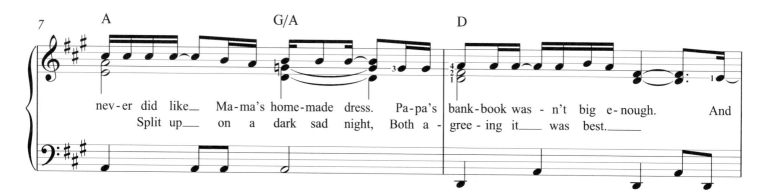

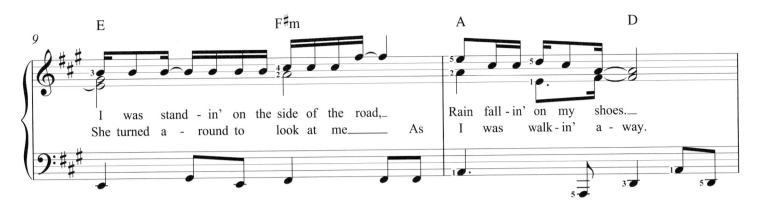

I was stand - in' on the side of the road,
She turned a - round to look at me

Rain fall - in' on my shoes.
As I was walk - in' a - way.

Head - ing out for the East Coast. Lord
I heard her say o - ver my shoul - der "We'll

knows I've paid some dues
meet a - gain some - day

get - tin' through.
on the av - e - nue."

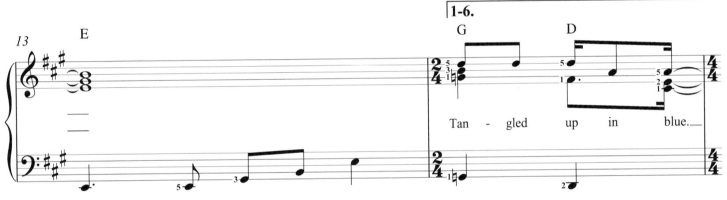

1-6.

Tan - gled up in blue.

7.

Tan - gled up in blue.

See following page for additional lyrics.

Verse 3
I had a job in the great north woods
Working as a cook for a spell
But I never did like it all that much
And one day the ax just fell
So I drifted down to New Orleans
Where I happened to be employed
Workin' for a while on a fishin' boat
Right outside of Delacroix
But all the while I was alone
The past was close behind
I seen a lot of women
But she never escaped my mind, and I just grew
Tangled up in blue

Verse 4
She was workin' in a topless place
And I stopped in for a beer
I just kept lookin' at the side of her face
In the spotlight so clear
And later on as the crowd thinned out
I's just about to do the same
She was standing there in back of my chair
Said to me, "Don't I know your name?"
I muttered somethin' underneath my breath
She studied the lines on my face
I must admit I felt a little uneasy
When she bent down to tie the laces of my shoe
Tangled up in blue

Verse 5
She lit a burner on the stove
And offered me a pipe
"I thought you'd never say hello," she said
"You look like the silent type"
Then she opened up a book of poems
And handed it to me
Written by an Italian poet
From the thirteenth century
And every one of them words rang true
And glowed like burnin' coal
Pourin' off of every page
Like it was written in my soul from me to you
Tangled up in blue

Verse 6
I lived with them on Montague Street
In a basement down the stairs
There was music in the cafés at night
And revolution in the air
Then he started into dealing with slaves
And something inside of him died
She had to sell everything she owned
And froze up inside
And when finally the bottom fell out
I became withdrawn
The only thing I knew how to do
Was to keep on keepin' on like a bird that flew
Tangled up in blue

Verse 7
So now I'm goin' back again
I got to get to her somehow
All the people we used to know
They're an illusion to me now
Some are mathematicians
Some are carpenters' wives
Don't know how it all got started
I don't know what they're doin' with their lives
But me, I'm still on the road
Headin' for another joint
We always did feel the same
We just saw it from a different point of view
Tangled up in blue

Make You Feel My Love

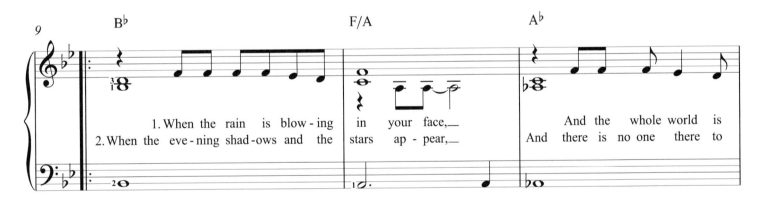

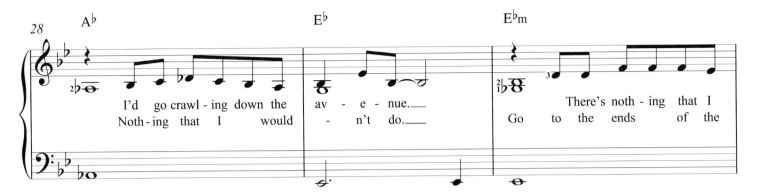

I'd go crawl - ing down the av - e - nue.___
Noth - ing that I would -n't do.___

There's noth - ing that I
Go to the ends of the

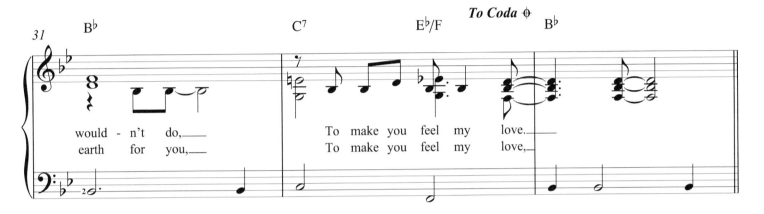

To Coda

would - n't do,___
earth for you,___

To make you feel my love.
To make you feel my love,

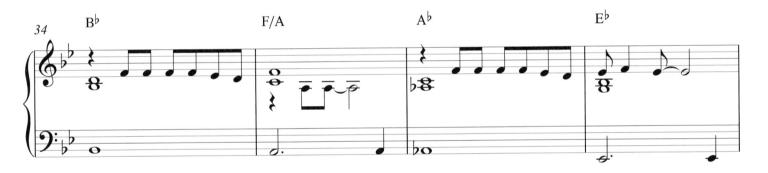

D.S. al Coda

would - n't do,
To make you feel my love.

Coda

rit.

to make you feel my love.___

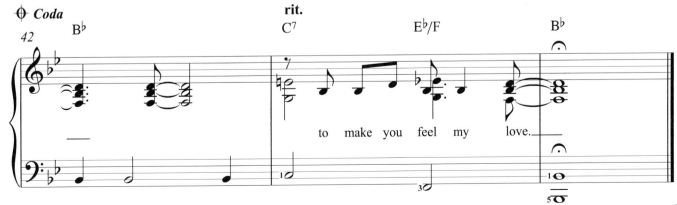

The Times They Are A-Changin'

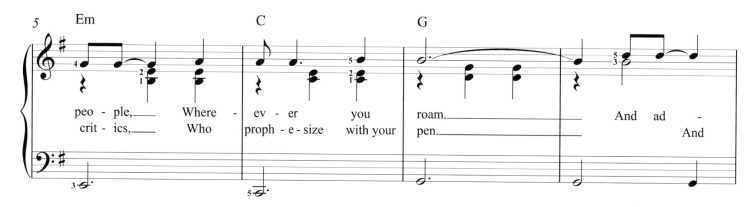

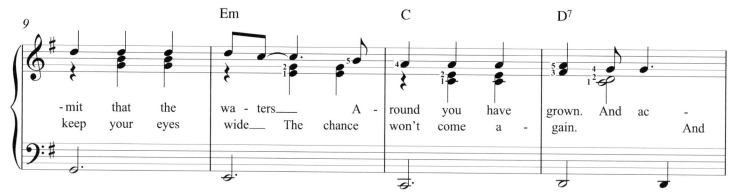

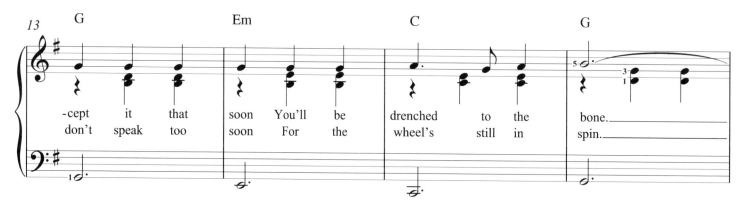

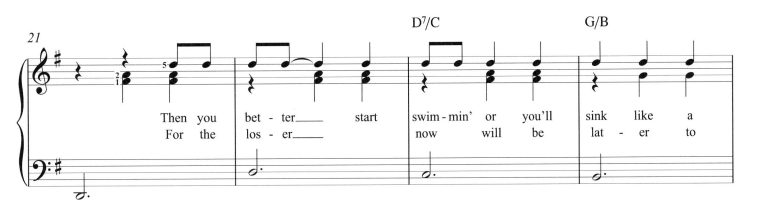

See following page for additional lyrics.

Verse 3

Come senators, congressmen
Please heed the call
Don't stand in the doorway
Don't block up the hall
For he that gets hurt
Will be he who has stalled
There's a battle outside and it is ragin'
It'll soon shake your windows and rattle your walls
For the times they are a-changin'

Verse 4

Come mothers and fathers
Throughout the land
And don't criticize
What you can't understand
Your sons and your daughters
Are beyond your command
Your old road is rapidly agin'
Please get out of the new one if you can't lend your hand
For the times they are a-changin'

Verse 5

The line it is drawn
The curse it is cast
The slow one now
Will later be fast
As the present now
Will later be past
The order is rapidly fadin'
And the first one now will later be last
For the times they are a-changin'